50 Quick and Brilliant Teaching Games

By Mike Gershon

About the Author

Mike Gershon is a teacher, trainer and writer. He is the author of twenty books on teaching, learning and education, including a number of bestsellers, as well as the co-author of one other. Mike's online resources have been viewed and downloaded more than 2.5 million times by teachers in over 180 countries and territories. He is a regular contributor to the Times Educational Supplement and has created a series of electronic CPD guides for TES PRO. Find out more, get in touch and download free resources at www.mikegershon.com

Training and Consultancy

Mike is an expert trainer whose sessions have received acclaim from teachers across England. Recent bookings include:

- *Improving Literacy Levels in Every Classroom*, St Leonard's Academy, Sussex

- *Growth Mindsets, Effective Marking and Feedback* Ash Manor School, Aldershot

- *Effective Differentiation,* Tri-Borough Alternative Provision (TBAP), London

Mike also works as a consultant, advising on teaching and learning and creating bespoke materials for schools. Recent work includes:

- *Developing and Facilitating Independent Learning,* Chipping Norton School, Oxfordshire

- *Differentiation In-Service Training,* Charles Darwin School, Kent

If you would like speak to Mike about the services he can offer your school, please get in touch by email: mike@mikegershon.com

Other Works from the Same Authors

Available to buy now on Amazon:

How to use Differentiation in the Classroom: The Complete Guide

How to use Assessment for Learning in the Classroom: The Complete Guide

How to use Questioning in the Classroom: The Complete Guide

How to use Discussion in the Classroom: The Complete Guide

How to Teach EAL Students in the Classroom: The Complete Guide

More Secondary Starters and Plenaries

Secondary Starters and Plenaries: History

Teach Now! History: Becoming a Great History Teacher

The Growth Mindset Pocketbook (with Professor Barry Hymer)

How to be Outstanding in the Classroom

Also available to buy now on Amazon, the entire 'Quick 50' Series:

50 Quick and Brilliant Teaching Ideas

50 Quick and Brilliant Teaching Techniques

50 Quick and Easy Lesson Activities

50 Quick Ways to Help Your Students Secure A and B Grades at GCSE

50 Quick Ways to Help Your Students Think, Learn, and Use Their Brains Brilliantly

50 Quick Ways to Motivate and Engage Your Students

50 Quick Ways to Outstanding Teaching

50 Quick Ways to Perfect Behaviour Management

50 Quick and Brilliant Teaching Games

50 Quick and Easy Ways to Outstanding Group Work

50 Quick and Easy Ways to Prepare for Ofsted

50 Quick and Easy Ways Leaders can Prepare for Ofsted

About the Series

The 'Quick 50' series was born out of a desire to provide teachers with practical, tried and tested ideas, activities, strategies and techniques which would help them to teach brilliant lessons, raise achievement and engage and inspire their students.

Every title in the series distils great teaching wisdom into fifty bite-sized chunks. These are easy to digest and easy to apply – perfect for the busy teacher who wants to develop their practice and support their students.

Acknowledgements

As ever I must thank all the fantastic colleagues and students I have worked with over the years, first while training at the Institute of Education, Central Foundation Girls' School and Nower Hill High School and subsequently while working at Pimlico Academy and King Edward VI School in Bury St Edmunds.

Thanks also to Alison and Andrew Metcalfe for a great place to write and finally to Gordon at KallKwik for help with the covers.

Table of Contents

Anagrams

Crosswords

Word Searches

Logic Puzzles

Number Puzzles

Keyword Bingo

Hangman

List It!

Screwed Up

Show me the answer!

Odd One Out

Make It!

Mastermind

Break the Code

Jeopardy

Zip, Zap, Boing

Wink Murder

Find the Answer

Dominoes

Line Up

Spelling Bee

You Say, We Pay

Word Master

Introduction

Welcome to '50 Quick and Brilliant Teaching Games.'

This book is packed full of fun, engaging and motivational teaching games for use across the curriculum and the age ranges. Whether you want to energise your class, help students to think carefully about big ideas or simply inject a bit of variety into your lessons, the games in this book will give you the practical tools you need.

All the games are easy to use – you can drop them into your lessons with the minimum of effort and fuss. They are also all fun and engaging – the perfect tools to motivate your students and get them excited about learning.

So read on and enjoy! But, most of all, I hope you have a fantastic time trying these games out with your students.

Play the Teacher

01 This game works well at the start or end of a lesson. In the first case, you can use it to help pupils revise the content they learned previously. In the second case, you can use it as a plenary to go back over what has been done during the lesson.

Split the class into two groups. Indicate that each group should come up with five questions they want to use to test the other half of the class. These questions should be about the topic you have been studying.

When sufficient time has passed, invite each group to select a leader. Group One sends their leader up to the front. They step into the teacher's shoes and ask Group Two their five questions.

Next, repeat the process but with Group Two's leader coming up to the front of the class.

It is great fun for students to take on the role of the teacher. You can repeat the activity over time using the same teams. If you keep track of the scores, this will help to develop a sense of competition as well.

Sit Down in Order

02 This game doesn't involve any lesson content. However, it is great fun and, as such, a good way to get pupils engaged, motivated and re-energised. It also requires careful teamwork and active listening.

All the students in the class stand up. Their aim is to all sit down again. But there is a catch!

Pupils must sit down one at a time. They must also say the number they are as they sit down. So, for example, the first person to sit down says: 'One.' The second person to sit down says: 'Two.' And so on.

Pupils are not allowed to communicate while this process is happening. If any students try to sit down at the same time or speak at the same time, the whole class stands up and the game begins again.

Students will have to work hard as a group if they are all to sit back down!

Last Answer

03 This is a fun little game which involves pupils responding to a question with the answer to the previous question. Here's an example in which the topic of study is human rights:

Question 1: What is the UDHR? **The pupil does not respond**

Question 2: What war lead to the UDHR being created? **The Universal Declaration of Human Right**

Question 3: Can you name one human right? **World War Two**

Question 4: What does inalienable mean? **The right to family life**

Question 5: How many human rights are on the UDHR? **It means it can't be challenged or argued with**

As you can see, the student has to hold the answer to the previous question in their mind while also processing the present question.

You can play this game with the teacher asking the questions or you can invite pupils to work in pairs and take it in turns to ask the questions.

Twenty Questions

04 In this classic game, the teacher selects something connected to the topic and the class then have twenty questions through which to ascertain what that thing is. Their questions can only be answered with the word 'yes' or the word 'no'.

For example, if the topic is migration the teacher might select the keyword 'refugee.'

The teacher would tell the class that they have selected a word connected to the topic, but no more.

Pupils then have to ask a series of yes/no questions to try to work out what this keyword is. If they can correctly guess it inside twenty questions, they are the winners. If they fail to do so, the teacher wins!

The game can also be played in pairs or groups, with students taking on the role of the teacher.

Question Race

05 Here is a simple way to enliven any activity where you need students to answer a series of questions.

Divide the class into groups of three. Create seven questions connected to the topic. Write each question on a slip of paper and make copies of these. You need to have enough slips for one per group per question.

Explain that the aim of the game is to answer all seven questions as accurately and as quickly as possible. You might want to give specific success criteria for the answers, such as: 'They must be a minimum of six lines in length.'

Next, give each group a copy of question one. Explain that, once groups have answered the question, they must send one member to the front of the class. Here, they show the teacher their answer. If the teacher is happy with the answer, the pupil is given question two, which they take back to their group.

The process repeats until one group has answered all seven questions correctly.

Dingbats

06 Dingbats are visual puzzles which convey the meaning of a word or phrase. For example, the word 'HAND' with an arrow pointing beneath it. This would mean 'Underhand' (because the arrow is under the word 'hand'). For more examples of dingbats, see www.kensdingbats.co.uk.

Dingbats are great to use at the start of a lesson. Display a few on the board and challenge your students to work out what they mean. You can use general dingbats or you can devise some connected to the topic you are teaching.

A second way to use dingbats involves asking your students to come up with their own. They can then try these out on each other. Alternatively, invite a succession of pupils to the front of the room to try their dingbats out on the whole class.

Teacher Quiz

07 An old-fashioned game that has lasted because of its flexibility.

Create a quiz you can use to test your students. This could be based on the previous lesson, the unit of work you are studying or the subject as a whole.

Students can work individually, in pairs or in teams. Pairs and teams help to generate a greater sense of excitement. This, in turn, makes the activity feel more like a game.

A nice alternative involves you providing the class with a series of ten categories (people, keywords, multiple choice and so on). Students select five of these categories and you then ask two questions from each. This method adds an extra layer of interest.

Student Quiz

08 In this game, students come up with their own quizzes.

Pupils can work independently, in pairs or in groups. They can then test their quizzes out on each other or on the whole class.

Sometimes students struggle to come up with questions. Help them out by providing a list of categories they can use.

You might also like to provide various sentence starters (which can be as simple as Who; What; Where; When; Why) or question types (multiple choice, definitions, problem-solving).

This game can be used as a plenary. Here, pupils work in pairs to produce five short and simple questions about the lesson. The teacher then selects two or three pairs at random who test the rest of the class.

A - Z

09 This is one of my favourite games. It's great for revision and also a good way to ascertain what students know about a topic before you begin teaching.

Pupils work in pairs. Each pair receives a sheet of lined paper. They write the letters A – Z, one letter per line.

The teacher introduces the topic (for example, World War Two or Animals) and explains that students have to come up with a word connected to that topic for each letter of the alphabet. The first pair to get 26 words are the winners.

Extend the activity by having the winning pair read out their answers while the rest of the class listen in and challenge any they think are not right.

Spot the Difference

10 Spot the difference involves close analysis, attention to detail and accurate discrimination between different items.

Examples of spot the difference games include:

- Two pictures

- Two pieces of writing

- Two diagrams

- Two objects

- Two pieces of audio

In all these situations, students are examining the items in question carefully and critically. As such, the game helps to develop skills of analysis as well as a close reading of relevant content.

A nice example of how to use spot the difference sees students being given two texts, ostensibly the same. In reality, the second text has been punctuated incorrectly. Students have to identify this by spotting the differences with the first text, which has been punctuated correctly.

You can develop the activity by asking pupils to come up with their own spot the differences.

Who Wants to be a Millionaire?

11 The long-running ITV quiz show 'Who Wants to be a Millionaire?' offers a great template for use in lessons. Simply download a PowerPoint such as the one available at https://www.tes.co.uk/teaching-resource/Who-want-to-be-a-millionaire-3009846, input your own questions and answers, and away you go!

You can also set students the task of designing their own questions and answers. The group who produces the best set then get to run the activity for the whole class.

Blankety Blank

12 Blankety Blank is an old television game show in which contestants are given a phrase containing a missing word or two. The missing items are replaced by a blank space. Hence the name, Blankety Blank.

You can easily adapt the template for use in your own lessons. A PowerPoint is available at https://www.tes.co.uk/teaching-resource/blankety-blank-game-6095095.

Two options can be used in Blankety Blank. In the first case, students are presented with the phrase and asked to work out the missing word. In the second case, pupils are presented with the phrase along with four options. They must then assess which of the options is correct.

The Million Pound Drop

13 Channel 4 created the Million Pound Drop. Contestants begin with a million pounds. They are asked a series of multiple choice questions. Each question has four possible answers. Contestants place their money on the answer(s) they think is correct. They are allowed to choose between 1 and 3 answers.

If they get the answer right, they take the money placed on that answer through to the next round.

The game is good fun and can be easily adapted for any subject. You can find a template at https://www.tes.co.uk/teaching-resource/Million-pound-drop-interactive-game-6085666.

Either print out some images of cash bundles for students to use, provide them with counters (each representing £50,000) or ask them to keep track of their money by hand.

Blockbusters

14 Blockbusters is an old favourite. I even remember one of my teachers using it when I was at school (on an overhead projector rather than an interactive whiteboard!).

You can find an excellent Blockbusters template at https://www.tes.co.uk/teaching-resource/Blockbuster-Template-and-General-Knowledge-Quizzes-6111991.

The game is simple and a lot of fun. Divide the class in half. One group will be blue, one group white. Blues need to make a chain running horizontally across the board. Whites need to make a chain running vertically along the board.

All questions are based on a letter of the alphabet. For example: Which 'A' is a country in South America? (Answer = Argentina).

As you can see, it is easy to adapt the questions to any topic.

Play Your Cards Right

15 Play Your Cards Right is our last television game show for now. It was memorably hosted on ITV by Bruce Forsyth.

Contestants in the original show had to decide if the next playing card to be revealed would be higher or lower than the previous one.

This concept can be easily adapted for the classroom. An example template can be found at https://www.tes.co.uk/teaching-resource/Play-your-cards-right-game--decimals-and-fractions-6298004. In this case, the topic is fractions.

Examples of other topics you could play with your class are:

- Population of countries

- Length of reign of different monarchs

- Dates of events (was it before or after)

In short, anything involving numbers!

Pictionary

16 This is another one of my favourites. Pictionary involves students drawing a word or phrase while their partner or peers try to guess what the image represents. Letters and numbers cannot be used in the drawing. Nor is the drawer allowed to speak. Thus, the game is all about trying to decode the image.

Two approaches suggest themselves.

First, the class is divided in half. The teacher comes up with a list of words connected to the topic. Pupils from each team take it in turns to draw one of these words while their peers try to guess. A tally of the score is kept.

Second, students work in pairs. Pupils decide who is 'A' and who is 'B'. The teacher asks the 'A' students to shut their eyes. They then flash a word up on the screen. 'B' students have to draw this for their partners, who have to try to guess what it is.

Charades

17 This is the classic Christmas game where people have to mime a word or phrase while their team try to guess what it is they are miming.

Create a list of keywords connected to the topic. Divide the class in half. Each group sends up one team member at a time. The teacher whispers a keyword to this person. They then have to mime this while their team try to guess what they keyword is.

You might like to put a time limit on the mimes (say, one minute). Keep a tally of the scores. If you wish, you can allow the opposing team to guess the mime if it has not been identified by the time the minute is up. The team who accrue the most points are the winners.

Scattegories

18 Divide the class into groups of three or four. Display a list of categories. The game works best if these are a mixture of general knowledge and subject-specific categories. Seven is a good number. Here is an example from a History lesson (students have been studying the Industrial Revolution):

- Figures from the period

- Pop stars

- Keywords from the topic

- Things you find in school

- Events during the period

- Desserts

- Places connected to the period

Next, select a letter and ask teams to write down an answer which starts with that letter for each category. The first team to get all seven let the teacher know by shouting out. The teacher then checks their answers.

The game can be repeated with different letters. I have found that 3-5 repetitions work well.

Taboo

19 Taboo involves students explaining the meaning of a word without using the word itself. While this is happening, their partner or team has to guess what the word is. Here is an example:

Student A: It's like when you go out and it feels nice, not too hot and not too warm.

Student B: Mild?

Student A: No, not mild. It's more a word you would use to describe an area where it's not too hot or cold.

Student B: Temperate?

Student A: Yes!

As you can see, the game can be played in pairs or in two teams involving the whole class. Simply create a list of relevant keywords and use these as the basis of the game.

Just a Minute

20 Just a Minute is a popular Radio 4 comedy panel show in which contestants have to speak about a topic for one minute without deviation, hesitation or repetition.

This format can be easily adapted for use in school.

Invite a student to the front of the room. Indicate what the topic is. Explain the rules and ask the class to shout out if they observe any deviation, hesitation or repetition. If the pupil fails to speak for a minute, invite a second student up. Continue the process until the minute is complete.

Whoever is talking at the end is the winner.

This is a great activity to use as a starter or plenary. You can also repeat it two to three times with different topics.

Anagrams

21 Anagrams are word puzzles. Letters need to be rearranged to spell out a word. Here are some examples:

- Tee Cult = lettuce

- Sin Ride = insider

- Nag a Ram = anagram

A nice starter activity involves presenting students with a series of anagrams they have to solve either on their own or with a partner. The anagrams can be relevant to the topic or general. In the latter case, they will still serve to get pupils thinking and using their brains.

Extend the game by having students come up with their own anagrams. They can then try these out on each other or the whole class.

A final development sees the teacher handing out strips of paper. Pupils write their anagrams on these and the teacher collects them in. Anagrams are chosen at random and read to the whole class, who have to try to work them out.

Crosswords

22 Many websites offer free crossword creation services. Here are some examples:

http://www.puzzle-maker.com/crossword_Entry.cgi

http://puzzlemaker.discoveryeducation.com/CrissCrossSetupForm.asp?campaign=flyout_teachers_puzzle_crisscross

http://worksheets.theteacherscorner.net/make-your-own/crossword/

In each case, you enter your own words and clues.

Students can work on the crosswords individually, in pairs or in groups.

You can also ask your pupils to create their own crosswords, either in class or as a homework activity, to try out on one another.

A final option is to create cryptic crosswords, where the clues have to be deciphered in order to reveal the word. This is more difficult (both in terms of design and trying to solve them).

Word Searches

23 The educational value of word searches is not particularly high. However, students often find them very engaging. As a result, they can be a good way to build motivation (for example, as a precursor to a challenging problem-solving activity).

Free online word search creators are available at:

http://puzzlemaker.discoveryeducation.com/WordSearchSetupForm.asp?campaign=flyout_teachers_puzzle_wordcross

http://tools.atozteacherstuff.com/word-search-maker/wordsearch.php

http://www.teachers-direct.co.uk/resources/wordsearches/

Logic Puzzles

24 Logic puzzles are those puzzles in which a series of constraints are provided which must all be fulfilled for the puzzle to be successfully completed. Here is a simple example:

Five friends are having a dinner party together: Darren, Tim, Sarah, Mavis and Harley. Darren and Tim cannot sit next to each other. Two women cannot be sat next to each other. Three men cannot be sat in a row. Tim cannot sit opposite Mavis. How can the friends be arranged?

One answer would be: Tim, Mavis, Darren, Harley, Sarah. This fulfils all the criteria.

You can invent your own logic puzzles, invite students to create some or find examples online.

Number Puzzles

25 These are all those puzzles in which numbers play a central role. Obviously they are common in Maths teaching. However, you can use them across the curriculum as starter activities, warm-ups or brief diversions to re-energise students during the middle of lessons.

Simple number puzzles include sums of various sorts, completion of sequences and equations.

More complex number puzzles include code-breaking and Sudoku.

In addition, you can find plenty of one-off number puzzles online. For example: Find a number in which the letters which spell that number are in alphabetical order (answer = forty).

Puzzles such as this offer a nice diversion in any lesson, helping to keep motivation levels high.

Keyword Bingo

26 Create a blank 3 x 3 grid. Give a copy to each student in your class. Display a list of between 15 and 25 keywords connected to the topic of study. Ask pupils to select nine of the keywords to insert into their grids.

When everyone in the class has filled in their grids, remove the list of keywords.

Explain that you will read out definitions of the keywords. Students must listen carefully. They should cross off any keywords in their grids whose definitions they hear.

The first pupil to cross off all nine of their keywords shouts: 'Bingo!' The teacher then asks the student to read out their words. These are checked against the teacher's own list. If the pupil has correctly identified the words, they are the winner. If not, the game continues.

Hangman

27 This is an old favourite. It can be played in pairs and groups, between teams or between the teacher and the whole class. However it is played, the principles remain the same.

One person selects a word or phrase connected to the topic. They represent this on the whiteboard through a series of place-holders, one per letter. For example: _ _ _ /_ _ _ _ could represent 'red card.'

The guessers may only guess one letter at a time. If a correct letter is guessed, this is inserted into the clue. If an incorrect letter is guessed, this is written on one side of the board. A gallows is also drawn, one piece per incorrectly guessed letter (or incorrect guess).

The aim of the game is to correctly guess the word or phrase before a full hangman and gallows have been drawn.

List It!

28 This is a very simple game which is excellent for use at the start of a lesson or new topic. It helps pupils experience success and bring to mind all the knowledge they possess about a specific area. It works as follows:

Ask students to work with a partner or in groups of three. Indicate that there is a two minute time limit. Introduce a topic and ask pupils to list as many words as possible they know which connect to that topic.

When the time is up, ask teams to count up the number of words on their lists. The team with the highest number are the winners (though do check all their words are accurate!).

You can develop the activity by asking for more specific items than simply 'words.' For example: people, places, concepts, studies or themes.

Screwed Up

29 Divide the class into groups of four. Give each group a piece of A3 paper. Display a topic on the board that you have been studying (you might want to supplement this with a series of sub-categories). Explain that groups have 90 seconds to write as much as possible on their pieces of paper, about the topic.

When the 90 seconds have passed, ask groups to screw up their pieces of paper and throw them at the next group along in a clockwise direction.

Groups take their new pieces of paper, unfold them, and then have 60 seconds to add as much as they can about the topic. Repeat as many times as you like!

Two variations are as follows. First, give every student in the class a sheet of A4 paper and have them all play the game individually. Second, give different groups different topics to write about.

Show me the answer!

30 For this game you will need a class set of mini-whiteboards and pens.

Hand out the mini-whiteboards and pens.

Ask students a question and then ask them to show you their answer. They should do this by writing their answers on their whiteboards and then holding these up for you to see.

Increase the sense of competition by having students work in pairs or teams.

You might like to develop the activity by asking pupils to walk around the room with their answers trying to convince other people in the class as to why they are right.

Odd One Out

31 Odd one out works brilliantly as a starter or plenary. You can also use it within a larger activity. Simply present students with a collection of items connected to the topic of study and ask them to identify which is the odd one out and why.

An odd one out can be made up of anything. Examples include:

- Images

- Keywords

- Statements

- People

- Objects

You can decide in advance which item is the odd one out and why or, alternatively, you can leave this open. Pupils then have to use reasoning and evidence in order to persuade you and their peers why a particular item should be seen as the odd one out.

Make It!

32 Divide the class into groups of three or four. Give every group a collection of building materials. Examples include Lego®, play-doh and collected odds and ends such as packaging, loo rolls and egg boxes.

Explain to pupils that they will be using their building materials to make a series of things connected to the topic.

Announce the first thing groups will have to make and indicate how long they have to do this. When the time is up, survey the finished products and announce a winner! Repeat the activity as many times as you like, using further things connected to the topic of study.

Mastermind

33 Mastermind is a popular television programme in which contestants take part in two rounds. In the first round, they have to answer general knowledge questions. In the second round, they have to answer questions about their specialist subject.

We can take this model and use it when teaching.

Divide the class into five groups. Assign a specialist topic to each group. Ask students to research the general topic you are studying as well as their specialist topic. When sufficient time has passed, quiz each group in turn, keeping track of the scores.

This game works well if you quiz each team on their general knowledge first, then on their specialist knowledge. Doing so allows you to increase the tension and sense of competition.

Break the Code

34 Tsih is a cedo or, to put it another way, this is a code.

In the example, the code is that to reveal the message you must swap over the 2nd and 4th letters in any words that have 2nd and 4th letters (hence, tsih becomes this and cedo becomes code).

You can set your students all sorts of different codes which they have to try to crack. The whole process promotes analytical thought as well as problem-solving. What is more, pupils will experience a great sense of (well-deserved) success when they do manage to unlock a code.

Jeopardy

35 Jeopardy is a popular American quiz show. In the game, contestants are given answers and their job is to work out what the question is. Here is an example:

Answer: The longest of the South American rivers.

Question: What is the Amazon?

This game can be great fun in class. It also helps students to think carefully about their existing knowledge and to reason with care and precision (in order to correctly identify a question which fits the answer you have provided).

It is easy to develop the activity as well. Simply ask your students to come up with their own Jeopardy-style answers to try out on their peers.

Zip, Zap, Boing

36 The whole class, including the teacher, stand in a circle. 'Energy' will be fired around this circle. It can be fired with a 'zip' or a 'zap'. Students can bounce the energy back the way it came by using a 'boing.'

'Zip' means the student points at the person next to them (left or right) and says they word 'zip'. This passes the energy on.

'Zap' means the student points across the circle at another pupil and says the word 'zap'. Again, this passes the energy on.

'Boing' means the student puts their hands up and says 'boing'. This bounces the energy back at the person who sent it.

The energy must be passed on correctly and as quickly as possible. Any pupil who is too slow or who tries to pass the energy on incorrectly must sit down. The last two pupils standing are the winners.

Wink Murder

37 Students stand in a circle. One person is sent out of the room. They are the detective. Meanwhile, the teacher selects one or two pupils who will be the 'murderers'.

These students must try to 'kill off' all their peers before the detective catches them. They 'kill' people by winking at them. If a student finds themselves winked at by the murderer, they must stage a dramatic death.

The detective re-enters the room and stands in the middle of the circle. They must identify the murderer before everyone is killed. They are allowed a maximum of three guesses. When the game has run its course, play on by choosing new students to be the detective and murderer.

Find the Answer

38 This game is an excellent means through which to elicit information concerning what students know about certain topics. It works as follows:

Stick five pieces of A4 paper up around your room. These should each have one of the following letters on them: A, B, C, D, E.

Ask students to stand up. Display a question on the board connected to the topic along with five possible answers. These should be labelled A, B, C, D and E.

Explain to pupils that they must find the answer by moving to the letter which they think is correct. When all students have moved, quiz two or three on the reasons for their choice.

Repeat the game with as many questions as you like.

Dominoes

39 Create a class set of dominoes. Each should have a question on one end and an answer on the other. The answers should connect to one of the other questions. All the questions and answers should connect to the topic of study.

Hand the dominoes out to your students and then...away they go!

Pupils have to connect all the answers and questions together so as to form a continuous chain encompassing all the dominoes.

The game promotes communication and team work. It also encourages students to think carefully about the topic in question.

Line Up

40 A fun little game that doesn't have much educational merit but which is great for energising a tired class or for bringing a bit of enthusiasm and motivation into the room.

Ask pupils to stand up.

Explain that they have to line themselves up in height order at the back of the room.

When they have done this, ask them to line up according to their birthdays. When they are finished, go along the line and ask each pupil to shout out their birthday. This will allow you to check whether the class have been successful.

Next, ask students to line up according to their shoe sizes. Except, this time, they aren't allowed to speak! As you can see, you can make the game increasingly challenging by introducing further constraints and changing the criteria by which pupils need to line up.

Spelling Bee

41 An old fashioned game this, but one which retains its appeal (and which is particularly useful when teaching keywords).

Give your students a list of spellings to learn (preferably connected to the topic of study!). Invite pupils to the front of the class and ask them to spell a number of these words, one at a time. Any student who incorrectly spells a word drops out. The winner is the pupil who continues spelling words correctly longer than anyone else.

You can alter the game by introducing a sponge ball. Throw this to a pupil in your class. When they catch it, give them a word to spell. If they spell it correctly, they get to throw the ball on and ask the person who catches it to spell another word. And so on.

You Say, We Pay

42 A game which I came across while watching Richard and Judy's Channel 4 program some years ago.

Create a series of PowerPoint slides containing words connected to the topic. One student comes to the front of the room and sits with their back to the whiteboard.

Set up the PowerPoint so that the first word is displayed on the board.

The pupil has one minute to try to identify as many of the words as possible. They do this by listening to the rest of the class, who can see the words but are not allowed to use the words when describing them.

So, for example, the word 'mountain' might be displayed on the board. Students would then say something like: 'really big rock sticking out of the ground that can go miles into the air, examples include Everest and K2.' The pupil would have to identify the word 'mountain' from this description.

As soon as the student has correctly identified a word, move the PowerPoint on to the next slide. You might also like to give them the opportunity to pass on a word if they become stuck.

Word Master

43 Display a long word on the board and challenge pupils to make as many words as possible using the letters contained within that word. Students can work individually or in pairs. You should set a time limit – 90 seconds to two minutes usually works well.

The winner is the pupil or pair who creates the largest number of words from the long word.

Listen and Draw

44 This game really promotes active listening skills. It also places the onus on students to think carefully about the words they use and about the way in which they communicate meaning.

Pupils work in pairs. They sit back to back. One student in each pair receives a blank sheet of A4 paper, a pencil and something to lean on. The other pupil gets a hand-out containing an image.

The second student must explain to the first student what is on their hand-out such that the first pupil can draw it. The aim is to recreate the original image as accurately as possible (the results can sometimes be hilarious!).

Definition Match

45 Here's a really simple game.

Display a series of definitions and keywords on the board. Ask students to match them up. Pupils can work in pairs or on their own.

And here are three ways to develop the game:

- Display a mismatched number of definitions and keywords.

- Jumble up the keywords so that students first have to unscramble the letters.

- Provide incorrect definitions and keywords. Students have to correct these first, then match them up.

Homework Games

46 One of the key features common to all teaching games is that they introduce an element of fun. This helps to raise motivation. It also asks students to reconceptualise the nature of learning.

You can extend this to homework. Instead of setting pupils a specific task to do outside of class, find an online game which is relevant to your subject and ask them to spend 20-30 minutes playing it.

Follow up in the next lesson by asking 3 or 4 students to share their experiences of playing the game with the rest of the class.

Online Games

47 An excellent website for online games is www.classtools.net. This brilliant site allows you to create free games, quizzes and activities using a wide range of ready-made templates. You can also invite students to create games of their own using the site.

Another good site is www.teachingenglish.org.uk, created by the British Council and the BBC. The games and resources on here are concerned with teaching English. Therefore, they are not appropriate for all teachers.

However, even if you do not teach English, you can still use the site as a means through which to get ideas for your own subject. Simply look through the various games available and think about how these could translate to the teaching of different topics.

Our third and final website for teaching games is www.bbc.co.uk/learning. This site contains a wealth of resources for students and teachers. There are many games to be found connecting to various topics on the primary and secondary curriculums. Type your topic into the search box and see what you can find.

Roll the Dice

48 This game combines luck and skill, making for a compelling prospect.

Divide the class into groups of four. Give each group a number or ask them to come up with a team name. You should have a list of questions ready, each of which should be connected to the topic of study. You will also need a dice.

Begin the game by asking Group One the first question. If the team get the question right, pass them the dice and ask them to roll it. The number which comes up is the number of points that team scores.

As you can see, there is potential for some unusual scoring to take place during the game!

Repeat the process for a set number of rounds of questions (five works well) and don't forget to keep track of the scores.

Human Bingo

49 Here's a great game which gets students up and moving around.

Create an A4 sheet of paper containing sixteen boxes. In each box there should be a question connected to the topic. Give each pupil in the class a copy of the sheet.

Explain that students need to move around the room and find someone who can answer each of the questions on their sheet. Pupils must find a different person to answer each question. When they have found someone, that person writes their name in the appropriate box.

The winner is the first student to get all sixteen of their boxes signed by different pupils. When this happens, they shout out: 'Bingo!'

The teacher then checks their sheet by reading off the questions and asking for the answers from the pupils who wrote their names.

Interactive Whiteboards (IWBs)

50 We conclude our journey through 50 quick and brilliant teaching games by thinking about interactive whiteboards. These offer a range of opportunities for creating and developing games either yourself or in partnership with your students.

In addition, the sites which serve the various software platforms connected to interactive whiteboards provide a means by which to share materials. Therefore, you may well find a great game which another teacher has already created – saving you time in the process!

If you can book a computer room, you might even like to set your class off on a game-creation task using your IWB software. This will see them thinking carefully about the content of the topic in order to include this as part of a successful IWB game.

And with that we conclude our journey.

The only thing left for me to say is: I hope you and your students have fun using the games!

A Brief Request

If you have found this book useful I would be delighted if you could leave a review on Amazon to let others know.

If you have any thoughts or comments, or if you have an idea for a new book in the series you would like me to write, please don't hesitate to get in touch at mike@mikegershon.com.

Finally, don't forget that you can download all my teaching and learning resources for **FREE** at www.mikegershon.com.

Printed in Great Britain
by Amazon